A WORKBOOK FOR FIRST PHILOSOPHY

Getting Started with Metaphysics and Epistemology

Douglass McFerran
Los Angeles Pierce College

I dedicate this to the memory of my own instructors, first the Jesuits at Gonzaga University who introduced me to Thomas Aquinas and later the professors at the University of California at Santa Barbara who brought me up to the twentieth century.

ISBN: 9781731446251

A NOTE TO THOSE USING THIS BOOK

I think of philosophy as a continuing conversation about what we can know about ourselves and the world that could possibly be more than just a set of beliefs or opinions.   In the West we look back to Plato who gave us the image of Socrates challenging the so-called wise men of his time in order to escape the relativism he saw corrupting political life.   With Plato's own student Aristotle, who coined the term "first philosophy" to describe what medieval followers saw as "the great chain of being," we find an effort to get at what makes the world of our sensory experience even possible.

The development of modern science challenged everything that had been medieval philosophy, especially when it came to talking about God and personal immortality. Descartes attempted to restore a sense of certainty through an emphasis on ideas that must be in our minds independent of our sensory experience, but this approach was rejected by Locke and Hume. The debate continued through to the twentieth century when a new generation of philosophers saw the proper job of philosophy as being an escape from what one of them (Wittgenstein) termed "the bewitchment of our intelligence by means of language."

This book, adapted from the material in an introductory course I have taught at Los Angeles Pierce College, reflects my own interest in the way in which the most important ideas we discuss all have biographies, typically focused on certain seminal writings.   They then reflect the cultural factors that impacted those authors and need to be taken into account.   This is why I have favored a more historical approach rather than just launching into a set of philosophical options (rationalism or empiricism in talking about knowledge, materialism or dualism or idealism in talking about reality itself) and calling on students to pick their favorites.

A key point I have tried to make in my own classes is that advances in technology have made the old questions debated by philosophers from

Plato onward newly relevant. Fifty years ago the possibility of successful heart transplants triggered efforts to have philosophers and scientists join together to rethink what we mean by death itself. What is happening today with advances in artificial intelligence in the same way calls on philosophers and scientists to rethink the links connecting the concepts of consciousness, legal personhood, and societal rights.

Ideally a beginning student would spend time with the original sources, and certainly this is the pattern with so many textbooks. However, those of us who make a living in the classroom realize that our students, especially at a community college, have neither the time nor the interest in taking on Plato or Descartes or Wittgenstein in their own words. In the classroom I do rely on audiovisual aids, especially material now available on YouTube or through Wikipedia, and I encourage readers to follow through on their own.

So is it the goal here for my readers to develop their own stands on any of the issues we discuss? Ironically, it does seem that philosophical progress is better seen when a student comes to internalize the point Socrates made when he said the god Apollo had called him the wisest of the Greeks because he saw the limits of his knowledge.

The workbook format is designed to suggest points for review as well as provide suggestions for written assignments.

Douglass McFerran
Los Angeles, November 2018

1. WHAT SHOULD YOU EXPECT FROM PHILOSOPHY?

Let's look at the official description of the course from the catalog at my own college:

> Students analyze some of the fundamental issues of philosophy and humanity that include topics such as knowledge and reality, the foundations of truth and science, and the nature of human consciousness/self.

Now this does not really tell you very much. Saying "the fundamental issues of philosophy and humanity" still leaves us hanging. Don't we talk about knowledge and reality in our science courses, whether it's in physics (as when we ask what is the world made of) or in psychology (as when we ask how we get to believe one thing rather than another)?

One common response is that philosophers pick up where scientists leave off. It is standard today to insist that science deals only with what can be observed and measured, and traditional "big questions" such as whether we have immortal souls or whether God exists are obviously outside science. But we do find them already being answered in our religious traditions, so just what is a philosopher supposed to do apart from making a case for one or another belief system (as in the grand tradition of Saint Thomas Aquinas)?

Now, professional philosophers (folks who get degrees and earn their living by teaching courses and writing books) insist that they play a special role different from that of the scientist or the theologian. Above all, they ask how our language itself is meant to work. Put as succinctly as possible, the great writers we look at from the past down to the present (Plato or Aristotle, Descartes or Locke, Ayer or Wittgenstein) keep hitting at what exactly are we doing when we say, for instance, we have or do not have immortal souls or that God does or does not exist. One way or another they are all thinking through what it means to be thinking.

Now this last paragraph is best understood only when you are already familiar with at least some of these writers. Quite a few years ago I attended an international conference in Montreal on teaching an introductory course in philosophy. After considerable argument, someone proposed that we would all agree a beginning student should be exposed to the nine most important names in philosophy, but (a dramatic pause) we just would never agree on the list.

Well, for this course on knowledge and reality let's take these nine individuals as starting points: Plato, Aristotle, Descartes, Locke, Hume, Ayer, Sartre, Wittgenstein, and the Buddhist philosopher Nagasena.

There will be material about when they lived and the factors influencing their ways of looking at things. But I will also attempt to make the course as real as possible by pushing you to look again at ideas you might otherwise just take for granted. Some of this might be personally uncomfortable, but at no point am I suggesting that any grade you receive in a course of this kind should on buying into one point of view rather than another. You would be expected to have your facts straight, and there should be improvement in your skill at thinking through the questions you are working with. Where you stand at the end, though, is not what matters. In fact, maybe being more confused or puzzled could well be a sign of progress.

A BIT OF HISTORY

An American philosopher, A.N. Whitehead, commented that all philosophy could be seen as a footnote to Plato, who lived in Athens twenty-four centuries ago. As a young man he had been someone hanging around Socrates, perhaps the most controversial figure of his time. Long before Plato was born, the playwright Aristophanes had written a satirical portrayal of Socrates as someone getting rich by teaching teenage students to mock their parents' values. In 399 BCE a jury heard charges against Socrates that echoed the play, voted him guilty, and ordered his execution.

Plato, concerned for his own safety, left Athens and traveled through other Greek areas in the Mediterranean. Some years later he returned, opening a school of his own and in a very changed political climate writing his own version of the trial and its consequences. Socrates now was presented as a model of someone searching for absolute truth at a time when traditional values, typically seen as having a religious foundation, were breaking down.

Plato was to write twenty or more imagined conversations between Socrates and various well-known figures of his time. The scope of topics discussed, as Whitehead observed, covered just about all the "big questions" that still make up philosophy. Aristotle, Plato's own student, in turn opened a school of his own and in very structured lectures presented a major alternative to the approach that Plato had taken.

> So what are examples of these "big questions"? Well, let's say we start with how we can be sure that the things we might believe about ourselves as human beings and our place in the universe are really true. This itself calls on use to see the difference between facts and opinions, knowing for sure and just having a belief. Right off this invites more questions about our minds, in particular whether there is something special that lets us see the very fact of thinking as setting us apart from whatever else exists in the world. Go on from there and we have whatever we might ask about "the supernatural" (personal immortality, the existence of God, even whether it makes sense to talk about the meaning of life itself).

> Plato presented a vision of reality existing at two levels, the world of our senses and another world that our souls would have seen before birth. This leads to a corresponding proposal for an

ideal society in which those who "remember" (true philosophers) would also rule over everyone else.

Aristotle rejected this idea and presented another technique of analysis that also suggested how at least some of us develop our full potential to know what is real and to live out the vision this suggests.

Jump ahead some twenty centuries to the beginning of our modern world. With the Renaissance lost Greek writings, especially the works of Aristotle (referred to simply as "the Philosopher" by Islamic writers), had again been available. At the same time advances in mathematics and science, especially those by the young French genius Descartes, invited a drastic reconsideration of both the big questions and the big answers. Descartes himself felt that he offered something missing with his predecessors: a logical method guaranteeing answers in philosophy as certain as answers in math.

Predictably, Descartes would be challenged, especially by the British philosophers Locke and Hume. Again there would be efforts to rethink starting points until by the early twentieth century a new movement would attempt to restrict philosophy by disallowing "meaningless" questions, understood as any that could not be dealt with scientifically. But that approach would not last, and serious philosophers did not hesitate to revisit how it might still be possible to ask some of the same "big questions" that had dominated debates in the Middle Ages.

SO WHAT'S GONE WRONG?

One famous philosopher wryly noted that the only thing he and his colleagues could agree on after all these centuries was that philosophers will always disagree. Here are a few possibilities about why.

- Our "big questions" cannot really be answered except through a revelation from God (the Torah, the Gospels, the Qur'an) or some type of enlightenment (Hindu and Buddhist teaching).
- Our big questions are essentially mistakes based on a confusion in language. This is a view promoted in Analytic Philosophy, as in the work of A.J. Ayer.
- Our big questions are finally about personal values, so there cannot really be objectively "true" answers, only individual choices. This is a view associated with Existentialism, as in the approach of Jean-Paul Sartre or, for that matter, Woody Allen.
- When asked about whether he really believed that the ghosts of his ancestors benefited from the grave offerings mandated by Chinese tradition, Confucius replied in effect that there was no point asking about such supernatural realities when the job was to straighten out how we deal with each other. This corresponds to the Pragmatic tradition linked with William James in which we think of beliefs as rules for action. On that basis what matters is the value of belief in itself.

AND WHERE DOES THAT LEAVE YOU AS YOU BEGIN THIS COURSE?

First off, I see my job as getting you to ask some big questions. In the process you will meet up with some writers who have definitely tried for big answers. This itself supplies some cultural background so that you have a better idea of what people are talking about when they use terms such as the Socratic method, a teleological approach (this has something to do with Aristotle), Cartesian dualism, or meaningless questions (from Analytic Philosophy).

I get to play Socrates, although I certainly hope not with the same results. If I do this well, I am getting you to think for yourselves, not just take something for granted. Yes, that might be dangerous at that. What happens if, even unintentionally, I undermine a system of beliefs that up to now have given your life meaning? If that seems to be a risk, it might be better not to take the course. You are the only one who can estimate your own fragility.

I do not, however, base your grade at any time on whether what you come up with as answers correspond to my own beliefs. What I can and will judge you on is how well you show you understand what we are talking about and how well you make a serious attempt to talk about it.

Finally, try to think of philosophy as a continuing conversation. It has been going on a long while, but because of that some answers as well as some questions that might have seemed reasonable once are now discredited. In a sense the conversation begins all over again with each new student joining in, but unless you are aware of what has been said in the past you are like someone trying to invent the wheel. We do try to build on what has been said already.

Right answers? That depends on whether we ask the right questions. And how do we know we are doing so? Well, we begin by starting with those "big questions" that seem to come most naturally. Then we see what happens.

SUGGESTED ASSIGNMENTS

1. Develop a short paper in which you look at the way we develop what we can be sure about in science. In particular, in a science course (imagine chemistry or biology) how do we know we are asking the right questions? How can we tell when we would have the right answers? Where does philosophy seem to be different?
2. Do the same exercise, only this time let's talk about theology or the study of what one is to believe in religious matters. Again, where does philosophy seem to be different?

WORKBOOK EXERCISES

In the space below write down a couple of sentences with your initial reactions to what you have been reading.

2. WHY SHOULD WE BE CONCERNED WITH "BIG QUESTIONS"?

Philosophers historically have asked the same questions that scientists would ask today as well as others that clearly do not fit into a scientific framework. Plato and Aristotle, for instance, followed the path many of their predecessors had taken in attempting to explain physical changes. For Aristotle, whose impact on medieval thought was so great that in the Arab world he was referred to simply as "the Philosopher" just as Muhammed was referred to as "the Prophet," there were four basic elements (air, fire, earth, water) that either combined or broke apart. That we no longer talk the same way (although it helps to know something about that old approach when we read someone like Shakespeare) is due to the rise of an experimental approach that combined with advances in technology.

One result of this basic shift was that we began to think of the other things Plato and Aristotle wrote about as better answered through religion if they are to be answered at all. Philosophers themselves for a while in the twentieth century tended to redefine the task of philosophy as establishing the guidelines for understanding science with all the "big questions" seen as "meaningless."

There are several reasons why this so-called analytic approach had faded. One has been the way in which technology itself has pushed us to rethink just what we can know about ourselves and our world. Perhaps the most striking example is how the possibility of heart transplants, possible only when the heart is still beating, called for a nationwide debate on the definition of death that resulted in the adoption of new laws so that doctors would not be charged with murder.

Questions about life and death can quickly expand. The advances in medicine that allowed heart transplants have expanded to include the possibility for radically altering how our biology works (detecting and eliminating certain genetic conditions, for instance).

At the same time we are moving rapidly forward in the field of artificial intelligence so that we can begin asking whether it makes sense to talk about machines thinking in such a human manner that IBM's Watson might just be the forerunner of a new species of life itself. Of course, much of this seems like science fiction, not anything to be concerned about. But then philosophers from Plato on have used what are called thought experiments in order to move our thinking forward.

So should we think of philosophy as offering big answers to go with the big questions? That certainly reflects much of the history of philosophy as a continuing conversation. The problem, though, is that when there are multiple answers, each supported by an acceptable line of reasoning, we seem stuck. This does not happen in mathematics and ideally it does not happen in science. We might expect it with religion and so we switch to talking more about belief than about knowledge.

British Philosopher Simon Blackburn acknowledges that what he calls "scientific triumphalism" has put humane studies such as philosophy on the defensive. So why bother? Perhaps as good an answer as any when he writes this: "I hope that the reasons at play at least raise some doubts and enable others to approach the difficult problems of how we do think and feel, and then how we ought to think and feel, with proper respect."

CAN WE HANDLE THE TRUTH?

Some years back Jim Carrey starred in *The Truman Show*, a film centering on the idea that for commercial purposes a baby is raised to adulthood on an elaborate set that simulates an actual world. The baby grows up thinking that all the people around him, including his best friend and his wife, are "real" and not just actors. Of course, in time he discovers the truth, but the question posed to him is why he should not be willing to accept the lie.

Plato anticipated the story somewhat when he has Socrates present what's been named the Allegory of the Cave. Individuals, chained from birth so that all they can see is the wall of a cave, watch the images of various objects projected on the wall as shadows. These to them are "real." One prisoner escapes, gets out of the cave, and sees the world outside. He eagerly returns to share his experience but is not only rebuffed by the prisoners still there but threatened with death if they were able to get at him. Unlike Truman, they prefer the world they know, even though in their case it is hardly an enjoyable one.

So here's the question. All of us have a more or less fixed set of beliefs, and that is true even if one of those beliefs is that we can never be sure what really is the truth. Socrates, wisest of the Greeks because he was so conscious of the limits of his knowledge, is not only commenting on a world in which "truth" counted for less than power but making us stop and think about the price we might have to pay if we really wanted anything different. After all, shouldn't loyalty matter?

We have looked at why Plato came to think the answer to the biggest question of them all-- how do we get at the truth?-- must already be there in our minds if we only asked the right questions. There is a meant to be a clear parallel between the escaped prisoner and the enlightened philosopher. Once you get the big answer (and let's add that you really "get it") you have a certain freedom that can be dangerous if you really think you are now called to get others to believe as you do.

LET'S TALK ABOUT A COUPLE OF THINGS FROM PSYCHOLOGY THAT MIGHT MAKE A DIFFERENCE

First is the case made by humanistic psychologists (Abraham Maslow, for instance) that we have a hierarchy of needs. Alpha needs basically deal with survival, beta needs with a sense of fulfillment. Thomas Aquinas, one of the greatest philosophers of the Middle Ages, expressed this with the adage that a modicum of comfort in necessary for the practice of virtue. Philosophy can readily be ridiculed as not being "real" and those concerned with it as "living in an ivory tower."

Second is an answer to why people continue to believe in something no matter how personally harmful it might be. This is how we deal with what is called cognitive dissonance. That expression originated with American efforts made during the Second World War to be as successful as the Nazis in the use of propaganda (surprised?). Actually, we were not at all as successful, which sent psychologists searching for what made the difference. The vital clue came when in the 1950s the Surgeon General's office came out with the report that cigarettes, which played such an important role in the American economy, had something to do with lung cancer.

In a long survey given to a great number of people, researchers had buried two vital questions: did the person taking the survey smoke and did the person think the government knew what it was talking about with the connection between cancer and smoking. Typically, those who took the report seriously were non-smokers and those who did not also rejected the report (not enough evidence, and so on).

What was happening? The new theory was that when two conflicting bits of information clash on something that matters, we have a situation rather like hitting two piano keys that are next to each other. There is dissonance, only this is in the cognitive (knowledge) sphere. We do not like it, so we tend to rationalize away the unpleasant information.

More research showed how this explained why gamblers who are losing tend to bet more heavily ("my luck is bound to change") because they cannot really accept that they are not winning or at least breaking even. It also explained why someone who was a victim of a high-stakes fraud was willing to continue with the fraud far more readily than would be the case if less were at risk. And it even explained why the fastest growing religious movements were those with definitely unusual beliefs in which new converts were required to attempt to convert others and were rejected, leading them to be even more convinced they were right and the rest of the world was wrong.

SUGGESTED ASSIGNMENT

Develop a short paper in which you look at the ways in which asking these "big questions" might benefit any student. Then think about the problem some students, especially those with strong religious beliefs, might have with these same questions. Finally, propose recommendations for anyone teaching a course of this kind so that those students with strong beliefs are not discouraged from full participation in class discussions. In particular, take a side on the issue of the extent to which an instructor should present his own views.

REVIEW QUESTIONS

What is this hierarchy of needs talked about in psychology, and how might it explain Aristotle's comment that it is useless to teach philosophy to young people because they are still caught up in their emotions?

What do we mean by the term "cognitive dissonance"? How might it explain what it means when someone says their mind is made up, so don't confuse them with facts?

In the film *A Few Good Men* Jack Nicholson, playing a Marine officer on trial, utters an unforgettable line about his interrogator not being able to handle the truth.   This brings out the conflict between loyalty and complete honesty.   Which do you think should be given priority in ordinary situations?   What might be examples of extraordinary situations in which you would reverse that order?

3.   WHAT MADE PLATO THINK THE WAY HE DID

Plato began writing about someone he had known when he was a very young man, and the first things he wrote were a version of the trial and then two episodes describing Socrates while he was awaiting his execution. This was already fifteen to twenty years after the events and at a time when Socrates' reputation had been rehabilitated so that he was now seen as a political victim rather than a dangerous subversive.

To understand where Plato was coming from, let's take a look at his description of an incident (maybe real, more probably just imaginary) that demonstrates an intriguing progression of ideas. It begins when Socrates startles Meno, one of his friends, by asserting that there is no such thing as learning, just remembering. To make his point he calls over one of Meno's slaves, just a child with no formal education, and has him go step by step through what today we would call programmed learning in order to arrive at the proof for a basic rule in geometry. Socrates infers that "if he did not acquire the knowledge in this life, then he must have had and learned it at some other time." That leads to the idea of our having minds that preexisted a present physical existence, and, of course, all that this suggests about the purpose of our even being here.

Wow, that is one very big idea. Built into it is the distinction between opinions and beliefs, any of which might be either true or false, and what would count as "real" knowledge with mathematics as a model. Remember the Pythagorean Theorem (you know, the formula that tells you that in any right triangle the sum of the squares on the sides equals the square on the hypotenuse, expressed simply as $A^2 + B^2 = C^2$)? It always works, but the goal of Euclid, who wrote the basic textbook for geometry a century after Plato, was to prove why it should.

Today few mathematicians themselves would share what's called an idealist position that what we talk about in geometry or any other branch of math somehow exists at a different level of reality. For Plato, there had to be something like the "Form" of a triangle-in-itself, and his argument (at least in his younger days) was that this world of Forms not only made "remembered" knowledge possible but was in fact the source of our everyday reality. All the mortal puppy dogs we see, for instance, are copies of some immortal "Dog" running around in this world of Forms, and all the pictures we draw of triangles are just copies of an eternal Triangle. This is not specifically a religious outlook, but in later centuries it became one when in Athens the last supporters of the banned pagan beliefs were the men who kept the school founded by Plato alive.

What it did mean for Plato, as he has Socrates spell it out, was that there was Truth (with a capital "T"). "Some things I have said of which I am not altogether confident. But that we shall be better and braver and less helpless if we think that we ought to enquire, than we should have been if we indulged in the idle fancy that there was no knowing and no use in seeking to know what we do not know; that is a theme upon which I am ready to fight, in word and deed, to the utmost of my power."

At his trial Socrates supposedly argued that he was indeed the wisest man in Greece because he knew that he did not know when all around him there were the self-proclaimed experts who readily said they had not just the big questions but the big answers. This was not a glorification of ignorance but, as we see from the quote above, a claim that we are "better and braver and less helpless" when we do keep going after the big questions.

WORKBOOK EXERCISES

As Plato develops the portrait of Socrates' readiness to accept his death, he keeps coming back to the idea of the immortality of the soul. In *The Republic*, the most famous of his writings, he also brings in the idea of reincarnation, which at the time was not at all part of traditional Greek religion. Compare this outlook with our more familiar Western notion of a state of consciousness after death in which "good" people are happy forever but "bad" people are suffering forever. Which approach would make you more likely to see Socrates as a role model for a student of philosophy -- and why?

One of the more interesting things about Plato is how as he himself gets older he has his Dialogues present Socrates as much younger and seeing problems with the theories Plato initially attributes to him. One of the best examples is Socrates having to back down on his first simplistic understanding of a world of Forms because of some commonsense objections. What do you think might be one or two of these?

4. ARISTOTLE RECONSIDERS WHAT HAPPENS WHEN WE THINK

After Plato's death Aristotle himself did a modest amount of traveling that included a return to Macedonia, where he tutored the young Alexander. The submission of mainland Greece to Philip of Macedonia, soon succeeded by Alexander, encouraged Aristotle to return to Athens and found a school of his own, the Lyceum. Here he remained until Alexander's death led to a new surge of anti-Macedonian feeling that threatened him also. In the years between he wrote, lectured, and supervised extensive research in the areas of biology and comparative government.

Plato, whose interest in mathematical thinking had been suffused with the mystic feelings of the Pythagoreans, had dismissed Ionian cosmology as suitable for after-dinner discussions but not for serious study. Aristotle, a born naturalist who showed little interest in formal mathematics, reversed this tendency in an effort, consistent with the empire-building of Alexander, to integrate all earlier attempts at scientific theory into one grand synthesis.

His own disdain for mathematics along with the Greek aversion to the tinkering that is the heart of any experimental method unfortunately prevented him from appreciating the weaknesses in the qualitative physics that he inherited from thinkers such as Anaximander, Empedocles, and Anaxagoras. He rejects, for instance, the atomic theory of Democritus on the basis of casual observations about the speed of a falling body in different media (arguing, then, that a body falling through the vacuum postulated by any atomism would travel infinitely fast--a logical impossibility), but he makes no effort to systematize these observations, a basic task that had to await the genius of Galileo almost twenty centuries later.

Aristotle's most fundamental disagreement with Plato centers on the assumption that the existence of abstract terms would be impossible without the existence of corresponding realities in a world of Forms. The error, as Aristotle saw it, lay in Plato's failure to recognize that the terms of ordinary language are often used analogously: the word "good", for example, covers a family of earthly meanings rather than referring to a single other-worldly ideal. Plato had developed an analysis of language that properly referred only to mathematics. Aristotle, less interested in mathematics, denied the validity of this style of reasoning.

This concern with meaning led Aristotle into a more far-reaching analysis of logic. Together with an exhaustive consideration of the varieties of a formal syllogism, these studies covered the types of valid and specious argumentation employed in public debate. Aristotle's interest in logic went beyond an impatience with sophistry or logic-chopping. His concept of science called for a presentation of evidence that would meet rigid tests of deductive reasoning. Logic, for Aristotle, was not itself a science, but it was a tool for science.

In his synthesis of earlier cosmology Aristotle reasoned that the process of physical change required a consideration of both the stuff (the material cause) and the structure (the formal cause) of any substance undergoing change. It also required a study of the factors inducing change (the efficient cause) and the intended result of change (the final cause). He resolved the problems raised by Parmenides and Zeno by introducing a distinction between potential and actual "being" (an acorn is potentially an oak tree, but it must develop this form to be the oak in actuality). All physical objects shared a common substratum of "first matter" qualitatively differentiated into the four elements of air, earth, fire, and water. These elements were capable of different types of organization as a result of the activity of things already having a specific form that could be shared: oak trees, for instance, produced acorns that were potentially new oak trees.

Sensory knowledge, for Aristotle, consisted in the communication of a form in such a way as to make the sensed object exist as a qualitative modification of the soul of the one sensing it. Intelligence was conceived as an internal operation by which the human mind, acting on sensory images, took on the structure of the physical objects known through sensation. Man in his knowledge could in a way become that which he knew.

Since intelligence was the distinguishing characteristic of man as a part of nature, any answer to the question of man's role in the world would have to be in terms of realizing his potential knowledge of the entire world. The objective fulfillment of man's nature--his specific "good" or his "happiness"--in a strict sense consisted in "contemplation," the acquisition of knowledge as an end in itself. Since the soul, for Aristotle, had its only reality as the form of a living body, this fulfillment was to be achieved during a man's lifetime--not after it, as Plato would have argued.

Aristotle, for all his stress on contemplation, is hardly willing to accept a Platonic withdrawal from society. Although man is what he is because of his mind, still the human being has both physical and social needs that must be met before he can be said to living a complete life. "Happiness" (our conventional translation of the Greek *eudaimonia*, which refers to far more than a state of mind) is itself seen as the activity by which man uses his abilities in conforming to the expectations of his society (the sense of "virtue"--*aretê*--as it is used by Aristotle).

Since man for Aristotle is above all the resident of the city-state (*polis*), he is a political animal whose greatest fulfillment is to be found in an active participation in civic affairs. While Plato is led to conceive of an ideal government as the benevolent dictatorship of philosopher-kings, Aristotle (for whom the purpose of government is to provide for the "common good," an order in a society that makes possible the good life of its citizens) is in effect arguing for what we today call democracy, although for both Plato and Aristotle this same word always has strong negative connotations.

The irony in Aristotle's analysis of society is that it is the depiction of an ideal already superseded by the fact of Alexander's conquests. The Greek world was now an empire ruled by a non-Greek. Aristotle and the Macedonian Alexander both shared the strongest reverence for the values of Hellenism, but Aristotle also maintained a contempt for the "barbarians" (even to the extent of justifying slavery as an appropriate means of humanizing non-Greek peoples) that blinded him to the realities of the changing Mediterranean world. Alexander, in contrast, saw the need for a high degree of both centralization and cultural fusion in order to achieve stability in his empire. Consequently, in Egypt he had himself divinized in order to claim legitimacy for his rule, and in Persia, the ancient enemy of Greece, he encouraged intermarriage between his officers and the daughters of Persian nobility, something that Aristotle regretted as a mongrelization of the Greek race.

This conservatism handicapped Aristotle even in his science. He translated Plato's Forms into the immutable species of his physics, and in so doing he backed away from the thesis of evolution put forward by earlier cosmologists and even by Plato. Aristotle's security depended on a vision of the universe as completely ordered ("a great chain of being," as his modern supporters have referred to it). The movements of the heavens (now seen as of an entirely different stuff than the earth in still another departure from Ionian tendencies) promoted physical change on the earth even while they in turn represented the efforts of still higher beings (pure intellects) to achieve the perfection of an ultimate Mind that blissfully contemplated itself in absolute immutability. This metaphysics, which attempted to naturalize Plato's mysticism, was to have an extraordinary appeal for later Islamic and Christian writers, and part of the history of modern science involves a manner in which the authority of Aristotle was invoked against investigators such as Galileo.

Aristotle's writings, as edited from various manuscripts and lecture notes by his followers, lack the literary grace of Plato's *Dialogues*. They do, however, sort out the questions of science and philosophy into categories we still recognize today. Many of his contributions, particularly in ethics (which he called "the political science") and the analysis of government, are still influencing contemporary thinkers. Despite his ethnocentrism and the static quality of his theories, Aristotle did attempt a resolutely secular approach to human existence. He offered the vision of a universe completely accessible to human penetration, and he also suggested, as against Plato, that it was the possibility of this penetration that allowed man his proper dignity in nature. Man's role is to understand the world and to act in his society in keeping with his understanding.

Greek thought reached its peak in the half-century between the founding of the Academy and the death of Aristotle. Philosophy found itself and attained a breadth and sophistication never again achieved in the West. This sophistication, paradoxically, was also the reason for the decline of philosophy in the centuries following. Plato and Aristotle were aristocratic intellectuals who overlooked the interests of the more common mortals in Greek society. As the empire of Alexander and his successors gave way to the empire of the Romans, very few individuals were able to identify with these ideals. Those who turned to philosophy were more willing to accept dogmatic teachings, such as those of the Epicureans and the Stoics, that also offered a detached way of life appropriate in an empire. Still others saw no reason to look to philosophy at all but instead sought salvation in a new set of mystery cults. The final episode of Greek thought in the Middle Ages will be as a useful tool for theology.

WORKBOOK EXERCISES

How would Darwin's theory of evolution reject how Aristotle talked about animal species?

Although Aristotle rejected his teacher's idea that we remembered rather than learned when we develop our understanding of the world, he did want to insist that what we experience could determine "real" knowledge of what things were in themselves apart from their surface appearances. What is the role of what he calls an agent (or active) intellect in doing this?

Plato has Socrates use his particular concept of the mind as a basis for talking about immortality. Aristotle does not accept the idea of immortality, so how would this affect efforts to interpret what the agent intellect actually was?

We typically translate the Greek word *eudaimonia,* which Aristotle uses in talking about the meaning of life, as "happiness." Why is this a problem?

5. DESCARTES STARTS FROM SCRATCH

In the early 1600s René Descartes attended the Jesuit school in his hometown in central France, then went on to get a law degree at the University of Poitiers. Galileo was already a notable Italian professor whose study of tidal motion appeared to support the still controversial notion that the earth moved around the sun rather than the other way around, and Descartes, whose first training in science would have been based on the work of Aristotle and his followers, would then have been caught up in this new way of doing science through experimentation.

The Jesuits, who accepted Aristotle's notion of a "first philosophy" as developed still further by Thomas Aquinas a few centuries earlier, would have taught him, for instance, how to prove that God existed and the human soul was immortal. Let go of Aristotle's science, though, and these proofs no longer seemed as convincing. It was a time to begin over, not just with science but with anything that was metaphysics.

He did this initially with a book called *A Discourse on the Method* in 1637, followed by *Meditations on First Philosophy* a few years later. The first book includes his presentation of what today we call analytic geometry, the fusion of algebra and geometry, as well as the basic concepts for his new approach to metaphysics. It is here that we first meet the classic phrase *"cogito, ergo sum"* (I think, therefore I am).

What Descartes had in mind by "the" method (for using our reasoning to get at truth in the sciences) was how he believed he managed to get at an infallible answer in the way that we might say a good detective would: by starting as a skeptic, breaking things down, seeing how the pieces fit together for a solution, then go through this repeatedly to make sure nothing had been missed.

- o *The first [step or rule] was never to accept anything for true which I did not clearly know to be such; that is to say, carefully to avoid precipitancy and prejudice, and to comprise nothing more in my judgment than what was presented to my mind so clearly and distinctly as to exclude all ground of doubt.*
- o *The second, to divide each of the difficulties under examination into as many parts as possible, and as might be necessary for its adequate solution.*
- o *The third, to conduct my thoughts in such order that, by commencing with objects the simplest and easiest to know, I might ascend by little and little, and, as it were, step by step, to the knowledge of the more complex; assigning in thought a certain order even to those objects which in their own nature do not stand in a relation of antecedence and sequence.*
- o *And the last, in every case to make enumerations so complete, and reviews so general, that I might be assured that nothing was omitted.*

But how would this apply to talking about God or immortality? This is what Descartes develops in his *Meditations*, which he actually dedicates to the Catholic professors of theology in Paris who he thought had been going about their job all wrong. If Plato had used imagined conversations as his style, Descartes reached back to the *Confessions* of Augustine. This great figure of early Christian thought attempted to get his readers to walk through his own thought processes, which we might call his meditations, as he moved from doubt to belief. Descartes starts off by presenting an imaginary set of conversations with himself that lasted for six days.

- *Day 1: He begins by trying to see if there was anything at all that he could not possibly doubt. A commonsense answer would be that we are certainly aware of our physical presence in a very real physical world. Descartes responds by citing what it feels like when we have very vivid dreams, then asks how are we to be sure we are not dreaming now. Even more, what if an evil demon had the power to create this state of awareness so that really there is nothing to awake to.*
- *Day 2: Ah, but one thing remains beyond doubt, and that is his mind is active even if he has no way of being sure he really has a body. He knows then that he exists, but so far only as a possibly disembodied thinker. "I think, therefore I am." The question now is just what kind of "thing" is the mind itself. He then tries to work through how being immaterial (unlike the body) it must also be able to exist without a body. At this point the concepts of "mind" and "soul" are used interchangeably, so he feels he has successfully proven the immortality of the soul.*
- *Day 3: The trick now is to see how to escape what we call solipsism, the idea that I exist but as far as I know I'm the only one who does. The answer is a review of our concepts until we find one that stands out in a special way. That is the idea of God as a perfect being (all-knowing and all powerful, above all). Descartes reasons (in what is called the trademark argument) that since we have no sensory experience of perfection, the idea could only have been caused by God implanting it in our minds so that we actually born with it (what we mean by calling this an innate idea).*
- *Day 4: Of course, we're still stuck with that evil demon hypothesis, so time out to think through how it is possible to*

know when we really getting at the truth of things. We work more with this business of seeing that "clear and distinct" ideas cannot be wrong.

- *Day 5: Back to God. The game now is to see that even imagining that God is imaginary means being not so perfect, so it is a contradiction for God not to be real (this is what is called the ontological argument). Now if we see that the idea of God being perfect rules out being a trickster, we can be sure God would not let us be deceived when we have such a continuous awareness of our bodies. We cannot just be dreaming.*
- *Day 6: We wind things up with a final development of the distinction between minds/souls and anything material, such as our bodies. This is the position we label as Cartesian dualism, which parallels what we have already seen with Plato.*

This, of course, is a very abbreviated synopsis, but it allows us to see how Descartes, like Plato, believed that through some completely mental process we can get at the most important truths for a philosopher: what we really are and how we fit into the universal scheme of things. This is the epistemological position of rationalism.

WORKBOOK EXERCISES

Descartes insists on an exaggerated degree of skepticism (what's been called a hyperbolic doubt) in his First Meditation. How does this compare with scientific reasoning today when we talk about a null hypothesis in research?

Much of Descartes reasoning depends on the concept that "clear and distinct" ideas have to be correct. Is this the same as saying that we have an innate guide to the truth built into our minds?

Thomas Aquinas four centuries earlier had presented five arguments for the existence of God based on the Aristotelian idea of there having to be an initial cause for motion (or action) in the universe (an "unmoved mover"). Central to his reasoning is that an infinite regress makes no sense as we look for a root cause in a chain. Why can't Descartes make use of such an idea?

Descartes sees benevolence as a necessary aspect of being perfect and so he rules out the evil demon hypothesis. Think back to our earlier reference to *The Truman Show* and the possibility that its creator saw deception as a necessary condition for Truman's continued happiness as well as the happiness of those viewing the show. Does this suggest God could be perfect and still be a deceiver for our own good?

What is the difference between the so-called trademark argument for the existence of God and the ontological argument that the idea of God necessarily implies existence? Which, if either, seems more convincing to you?

METAPHYSICAL LABELS

Philosophy textbooks, like textbooks for so many other subjects, tend to favor grouping various points of view into categories. One problem on doing so is that a student is tempted to think that using a label tells us all we really need to know about any point of view falling into that group. In American politics we tend to label people or positions as liberal or conservative, regardless of how moderate or how extreme their views actually may be, and we have seen how this discourages constructive discussions.

One example is the label "rationalist" as applied to Plato's way of talking about how we know what's real. For example, he has Socrates say that we never really "learn" something, we just "remember" it when given the right questions (the so-called Socratic method). Please do not confuse this use of the term "rationalist" with the view that beliefs should be based on reason rather than faith, as in a church's official teaching. The contrast is with a view that all knowledge has to grounded in sensory experience (no such thing as innate ideas), for which the label is "empiricist."

But how about categories of reality itself? Here I am not talking about an obvious difference between fact and fiction, as when we might have a novel in which the entirely fictitious Sherlock Holmes is meeting with the quite real Queen Victoria. Instead it is the idea that either there is just one type of reality or there are two types linked together. When we go for a single reality (monism), it will be either that of the physical world we experience daily and study in science (we call this materialism, not to be confused with the view that only money and material goods are important) or that of consciousness itself, what happens just in the mind. Making the mind real and the body and the physical world somehow an illusion is called idealism (not to be confused with how we talk about someone's values).

When we say bodies and minds are really different things (or substances), as when Descartes defines a body as something extended in space (*res extensa*) and a mind as a thinking thing (*res cogitans),* we are adopting the view of dualism. Plato with his world of Forms is certainly a dualist, and so is Descartes, although his split between mind and body stands out more sharply. This actually is what disturbed his Catholic critics, since it compromised how we might talk about doctrines such as the Incarnation, and his denial of consciousness to animals has not endeared him to animal rights activists.

Idealism is certainly more frequently found in Asian views than Western ones, but immediately after Descartes two prominent exceptions in Europe are Gottfried Leibniz (our minds are "windowless monads" with God synchronizing our experiences) and Baruch Spinoza (there is only one substance if we think in terms of independent existence, and ultimately our minds Just have to be ways in which God is real). Later in Britain there is George Berkeley (to exist is to be perceived, so our reality depends on God's awareness).

A general comment I will make is how Western philosophy, unlike its Asian counterparts, continually accepts certain concepts as so "obvious" that the terms are kept in play rather than rethought. From Aristotle on there has been this notion of "substance" as that which makes anything real regardless of its appearances. It is also what makes modern Western philosophy (what has happened from Descartes to the beginning of the twentieth century) seem so irrelevant to anyone used to thinking in terms of today's science. We will certainly see more of how the past hangs on in current debates about the mind-body relationship.

SUGGESTED ASSIGNMENT

Leibniz, Spinoza, and Berkley are all labeled idealists. Choose any one of these three and use an online resource such as the Internet Encyclopedia of Philosophy or the Stanford Encyclopedia of Philosophy to learn more about him. Then decide how we might think or act differently if we were to buy into that person's position.

6. LOCKE AND HUME BRING THINGS BACK DOWN TO EARTH

John Locke, born in England in 1632, was given what was then a traditional education at Oxford but found himself caught up in the new currents of thought coming from France with Descartes. He did not accept the Cartesian emphasis on innate ideas, and in the spirit of Francis Bacon decided to take a more experimental approach to the question of how we come to have ideas at all. This may help explain why he also increasingly took a strong interest in medicine. He made important connections in English politics through his work as a doctor, and soon he was caught up in developing a constitution for the colony in Carolina.

1688 was the Glorious Revolution, which marked a watershed in British politics as once and for all it was clear that it was Parliament and not the King of England deciding the law of the land. Shortly after, Locke published *An Essay Concerning Human Understanding* and *Two Treatises of Government*, both of which had a profound influence on both English and American readers, especially at a place like Harvard University. In time what was then a radical approach to what government was all about became the inspiration for the men who developed the new American republic.

Born early in the eighteenth century, David Hume became best known in his own country as having authored of what is still the standard history of England up to his time while working at the university library in Edinburgh. Philosophers worldwide know him more for a very early work that got barely any attention when it was published, *A Treatise of Human Nature,* and his later and more successful projects*, An Enquiry Concerning Human Understanding* and *An Enquiry Concerning the Principles of Morals.*

What makes him especially interesting is how, like Descartes, he wants to avoid taking anything for granted in the effort to establish how we can know who and what we are. Unlike Descartes, who thought he had found a way to escape even the most extreme possibility (being deceived by an evil demon in his sensory experience), Hume quite intentionally allies himself with the men who took over running Plato's Academy after his death. They came to be called the Skeptics (doubters) and insisted that any search for an absolute truth was doomed to failure. What should matter, they said, was to pursue peace of mind by conforming to what was culturally expected.

The march of thought in Europe had been from Cartesian dualism to the metaphysical idealism of Leibniz and Spinoza. Locke, as we shall see, is not convinced that we can systematically prove that our souls (or minds) are entities separate from the material world, but he will accept this anyway. George Berkeley, writing twenty years after Locke publishes his study of human understanding, goes much further and argues that existence itself is a matter of being perceived so that what we think is a material world could not have a reality independent from the mind of

God. This aligns him more with the idealist direction Leibniz had been taking.

Hume, twenty years further on, breaks step with this idealist tendency to explain our awareness of the physical world in terms of a divine consciousness. Proudly asserting himself as an Academic Skeptic, he revisits what Locke had tried to do but clearly rejects his predecessor's willingness to invoke much older language and a way of thinking that even allowed the reasoning of a Leibniz or a Berkeley to get started. In doing so, he invites us to look again at what was going on in the Academy at the time of Plato.

HOW DO SENSATIONS BECOME THOUGHTS?

Sophia is the Greek word for wisdom, but rather than claim to be wise (*sophos*) himself, the legend is that Pythagoras, mathematician and cult leader, preferred to say that he was a lover (*philos*) of wisdom. In part this may have been because while a number of Greeks had speculated on how nature worked, he was going to something deeper that suggested what we see as nature is ultimately to be explained through numbers and geometric shapes. Plato later on would keep this thought alive in some of his writings.

The key here is that the triangles I draw will have a lot of things I can say about them, but what I come up with as always the case (like the Pythagorean Theorem, which invited speculation about the existence of a world of numbers—radicals--that cannot be expressed with the same words we use to count) is not at all just what I see in my pictures. Plato came to say it was like having a line divided so that below would be the strictly visible things I see physically and above the abstract forms I "see" mentally.

Whatever we call reality could itself be understood the same way, a world of forever changing physical images below a line and a world of pure forms or shapes that are, as it were, reflected in the physical world. The human soul had the capacity to see both, but when encased in a human body, vision of what's above the line is dimmed like a forgotten memory. Students who wrote about their time in the Academy commented how Plato stressed a skill in mathematics (primarily geometry) as a prerequisite for anything else he would be talking about.

Plato's prize student was Aristotle, who as time went on broke with Plato's talk of inborn (innate) ideas as well as with his master's belief that what made someone "good" had to be recovered knowledge of some world of Forms representing moral qualities. After Plato's death, denied the chance to take over the Academy, Aristotle left Athens for a few years, then returned to found a school of his own. What he aimed at was a compilation of knowledge in everything from a skill in public speaking to a study of how nature (*phusis*) works to a "first philosophy" that students who edited his lectures simply listed as what came after (*meta*) this study of physics (metaphysics).

Where Plato might look more at triangles, Aristotle looks more at trees as well as all the other features of the world of nature. Some fallen acorns meet the conditions to become seedlings that in time might be full-grown oak trees. Kittens and puppies are born, grow to become mature cats and dogs that can become the parents of still more kittens and puppies. A tree, cat, dog, and every other living thing can be seen as an individual expression of what it means to be tree, cat, or dog. Each is something that can be seen as being a certain kind of object with a substratum of material elements assembled in a way that is like other objects looking and acting much the same. There are matter and form together, and with a living thing the form that directs how it comes to look and act can be called its soul.

Human beings can look out at trees, cat, and dogs and talk about them as representatives of their species. In doing so, the sensations that make up sight or hearing or touch are all at work to become ideas, forms reproduced in the mind, which is something within the soul or life force. Now where Plato wants to see memories recalled, Aristotle has to explain how what is outside in the world as an object gets to be represented inside our heads as a thought, specifically a thought that not only identifies the individual (Garfield or Marmaduke) but recognizes the kind of thing it is (a cat or a dog). Here is where he gets ambitious, developing a theory that should tie everything together. We have minds or passive intellects taking in sensations, but there also has to be an active or agent intellect processing them.

Aristotle might be delighted with contemporary technology to illustrate what he means. Imagine a camera set up to record individuals walking through a store. What is needed is a way of knowing who these individuals are, so the camera is connected to a computer that itself draws on a mainframe (let's talk about it as the cloud) where there is already a record of tens of millions of faces. The computer linked to the cloud almost instantly can report a match between Jane Doe and the customer browsing at the cosmetics counter, and Jane receives a personalized message on her iPhone about a special discount she can get on a certain brand.

Arab commentators on Aristotle were divided on how he had meant to think of an agent intellect. Does each of us have this processing ability built in, or might it be more like something leased from a single processor separate from us (like the cloud in my example)? Ibn Sina (Avicenna) thought we each had this ability, and Thomas Aquinas followed this interpretation to support his own case for the immaterial nature of the soul.

So we see Garfield at play and the distinguishing characteristics that mark his catness as well as his individual identity are "abstracted" from an outside world to become part of our interior mental landscape. In watching this particular kitty we do not, of course, observe the underlying nature of felinity--Garfield's enduring "substance"--but only what can change from moment to moment, those characteristics we call "accidents."

Talking about reality in terms of substance and accident set the linguistic rules at work from Greek times through the Middle Ages. Leibniz and Spinoza played with them in developing their own theories. But in England the new emphasis on an empirical study of the world (one based on what we can see and not on preconceived or *a priori* notions inherited from Aristotle) created the need for a different approach to the question of how images become ideas.

This is the task John Locke set himself. Crucial to his theory is an emphasis on the mind at our birth being like the blank wax tablet used by children in school in the days before pencil and paper. We start with a *tabula rasa* (an erased or blank tablet). Then from infancy on we have sense impressions that our minds begin assembling into our ideas. We learn to talk with words that are linked with sense impressions, as we see when child can point to a certain yellow cat in a television cartoon and say "Garfield." Eventually we move on to the very sophisticated ideas played with by philosophers.

Locke develops this encyclopedic analysis over several hundred pages. What is crucial is showing that we do not need to resort to a theory of innate ideas. As such it is meant as a definitive rejection of Descartes.

But there is one key problem that both Berkeley and Hume will exploit afterwards. How do we work from our sensory experience to ideas such as that of substance (unseen by definition) or causation? At some point in talking about the world our awareness of both continuity and change demands new linguistic inventions, new ways of expressing what we think we see happening. We take a number of "simple" ideas and make up new ones, such as the idea of a substance as shorthand of sorts to express what must stay the same about things and the idea of causation to express how things are changed.

Are we supposed to prove that there are "real" substances? No, Locke thinks it is enough to show why such an idea comes about as a result of our perceptions. Berkeley forces a stop at this point with his adage "to be is to be perceived" and then moves on to a complete idealism. Hume forces a stop as well, but denies that we can go on or that we even need to.

At one point, when he writes about a theory of government, Locke will just fall back on a notion of self-evident truths (language echoed in our own Declaration of Independence), and for practical purposes this has been at work all along. How else could we talk about how things change appearances but are still the same things? Just express the point about substances and accidents and we should be able to see why it is "true."

HUME RETHINKS THE QUESTIONS

Locke's discussion of how we think is five times as long as Hume's, but then Hume was less concerned about dismissing the notion of innate ideas. Hume, who often is seen as the forerunner of today's behavioral psychology, is far more disruptive. By coming back to the talk about our sensations, he tries to explain, as Locke did, how their remembered impressions get assembled together to be our ideas of trees and cats and dogs. But then, instead of going on to justify the other terms philosophers used in their metaphysical discussions, he reminds his reader of the limits in this process. In particular, by stressing the constant flow with these images, he attempts to wean his readers away from thinking they experience more than is the case. Do we experience substances? No, we just find this talk helpful and so get used to talking this way. Do we experience causality? No, we see one billiard ball hit another and infer the the first ball makes (causes) the second ball to move.

Today it is much easier to appreciate what Hume is saying. After all, once trained to think as scientifically we are used to thinking of all the things around us as reducible to atoms and the quanta of energy affecting them. The show that goes on in our sensory world is like the shadow plays in Plato's imagined cave. What makes the show possible is what modern science is all about, but the point is that we do not experience atoms as such and even talking about them as "things" misrepresents the situation.

Hume's most drastic revision is his challenge to the supposed supremacy of intelligence over emotion. Free will, he argues, is entirely an illusion. Reason, seen for what it is, should be viewed as the instrument our emotions use to look for pleasure and avoid pain, based on the continuing experiences of both. This emphasis on a pleasure/pain-based explanation of what makes us do anything is called hedonism (from the Greek word for pleasure).

This view of reason as an instrument also softens what could have been a so-called "hard determinism" (what's found with B.F. Skinner's behavioral psychology, for instance). Hume's approach, a so-called "soft determinism," has been labeled compatibilism to reconcile our everyday experiences of choice with how Hume explains what's going on, as it were, behind the scenes. It also is what allows him to develop a theory of the law (with his contributions now being newly explored in various conferences, especially in his native Scotland). Laws, with a corresponding understanding of crime and punishment, are meant to motivate individuals, whom Hume believes to be fundamentally capable of empathy so that they can appreciate the sufferings of others. By experiencing, even by seeing what happens to someone else, the consequences of breaking the law we are selfishly moved to avoid those actions which could lead to the same consequences for ourselves.

One point Hume strongly emphasized was that no matter how much we understand facts, we do not logically derive values from them. "Is" does not give us "ought."

Two centuries later a number of European philosophers built on a nineteenth-century idea that our ways of explaining the world had gone from a mythological stage to a metaphysical one and then to a "positive" one as science progresses. Calling themselves Logical Positivists, they talked about questions that could not be resolved through quantitative observations as "meaningless." Their key point was this distinction between descriptive statements (what we do or what we see) and normative ones (what we should do or what should be).

David Hume, had he lived to see the day, would certainly feel vindicated, even though he most likely would not have agreed that philosophers should keep silent when it comes to values.

SUGGESTED ASSIGNMENTS

Recommended for philosophy majors. The German philosopher Immanuel Kant credits David Hume with awaking him from his "dogmatic slumber." He then attempts to explain how the mind innately processes our experiences so that we can avoid Hume's skepticism. Again use the IEP or the SEP as online resources to learn more about his approach and present as clear a summary as you can.

Recommended for psychology majors. Do some research to see how much more do we know today about the way in which we form our ideas than we find in either Locke or Hume. Summarize what you have learned about the major differences. Then decide whether this means that it really would be a waste of time to read what either philosopher had to say.

WORKBOOK EXERCISES

What do we mean by the term "innate ideas," the starting point for a rationalist point of view? How is Locke's "blank slate" supposed to express an alternative for an empiricist point of view? Which seems the more acceptable to you?

Plato saw geometry (things like the Pythagorean Theorem) as setting a gold standard for philosophy. Descartes certainly agreed and tried to apply this to what we think of today essentially religious questions--the existence of God and the immortality of the human soul. Why did his own church then condemn his views?

We know Locke, unlike Hume, was respectful when it came to these questions but at the same time made the unprecedented case that a government should not attempt to impose any religious beliefs, even those of someone like the King of England (since the time of Henry VIII the official head of the Church of England).

What is called "hard" determinism (what we find in the behaviorist approach of B.F. Skinner) says that free will is an illusion since everything we choose to do depends on a combination of causal factors that we do not clearly see at work. Why does Hume's view of how we get our idea of causality rule out his being a "hard" determinist even though he insists that reason is only a tool for our emotions and not an independent factor in our choices?

7.   THE GHOST IN THE MACHINE

Descartes sparked a revolution in philosophy but, despite his claim to have proven such things as the soul's immortality and the existence of God with the same certainty we might have about the Pythagorean Theorem, he never felt the love, either from his church or from his country. He moved to Holland but died of pneumonia in Sweden when he went there at the invitation of the queen.

Philosophy itself moved on, as we've seen with Leibniz and Spinoza in Europe. In England his entire program of reasoning to absolute truths just by examining our own ideas came under attack with John Locke and then David Hume. In the twentieth century, with the rise of what was called Analytic Philosophy, Harvard's Gilbert Ryle put down Descartes' approach by saying his dualism made us just ghosts in a machine. If in fact there are two distinct types of reality with minds and bodies, how are they supposed to link up? Descartes himself thought of the mind as most probably acting through the pineal gland in the brain, but this begged the question of there even being the possibility of interaction. This was what had left the door open for Leibniz and his theory of monads synchronized by God.

Ryle went further by attempting to develop a quite different approach to talking about our minds. First, he made the point that there was a serious logical flaw right off in the *Meditations*. When Descartes says "I think, therefore I exist," he argues that he has shown the mind to be real quite apart from the body. The difficulty, Ryle says, is that this is the same kind of mistake someone might make when asking to see a college and is shown buildings and classes and activities keeps asking to see the college as though it is something in the same category as these other things being pointed out to him. It is the same kind of mistake we might make when we are shown poodles and terriers and collies but still ask to see a dog.

But saying that Descartes went off the tracks as soon as he begins talking about his mind as a though it is in the same category as his body (a category mistake, then) still does not quite answer the question of what it is we are talking about when we say "mind" and "mental activity." Ryle tries to answer this by talking about states or dispositions of the physical entity that is a body. Just as having legs that function as they should "disposes" me to get up and walk, having a brain "disposes" me to think about what I'm doing when I do walk, remember what I've done, or plan to do it again. Obviously I can walk and not be thinking about it since I am paying attention, say, to the scenery around me. And I can in fact not actually be walking at all but having a dream in which I am taking a stroll in the sunshine.

THE PROBLEM OF OTHER MINDS

Descartes himself had already drawn the conclusion from his identification of the terms "mind' and "soul" that anything lacking a soul (and as a good Christian he would accept that only human beings had souls) could not then be capable of thought as we have just talked about it. This would be a dog, for instance, just as it would be one of the automata or robots in the shape of a human being that clever mechanics had been crafting since the days of the Roman Empire. Any animal might, like a robot on display at a nobleman's party, give the impression of mental activity, but that's all it would be. Pull a dog's tail and it might howl in pain, but since it is a completely different entity from ourselves its apparent suffering should not bother us.

But how do we know that even other human beings have minds like our own? It might be very convenient to think some did not, and, tragically, as trade in African slaves took hold in the Americas it was quite easy for their owners to justify their actions by seeing their victims as not completely human. However, this still leaves open a very tricky question about how in fact we do know that the people around us -- some or all -- are not like the characters in Ira Levin's novel *The Stepford Wives*, clever copies of real people but actually just, as it were, machines without the ghosts.

Solipsism (from the Latin for "alone by oneself") is the position that we can only be sure of our own existence while the rest of the world is just a dream or, as Woody Allen suggested, we are just images in someone else's dream. Of course, "normal" people would never believe this, right?

But what if we switch how we look at the problem. Now I can be sure that there are other minds (good news, we're not alone), but they may not always go along with what we expect (bad news, we're not alone). Think of HAL in the film *2001*.

HAL is the ultimate example of AI (artificial intelligence), able to think enough like a human that "he" has an instinctual desire to survive on his own and so becomes a threat. (Imagine Siri on your iPhone deciding whom you should call and refusing to let you hang up until you do. Is it too far-fetched to think that by the time we hit iPhone 20 this could happen? Of course, she would be programmed only to do this for your own best interests, whether you appreciate that or not.)

But now we are going beyond talking about AI as simply knowing more and deciding better according to well-defined rules. To think humanly is more than just abstract cognition or calculated decisions, and the question should be whether this by definition is beyond any machine's pay grade. Let's see why.

WHAT ELSE MAY HAVE GONE WRONG WITH DESCARTES

In 1995 Antonio Damasio, whose field is neurology, published a book with the provocative title *Descartes' Error: Emotion, Reason, and the Human Brain*. His case is that from Descartes on we have been thinking of our minds just in terms of cognition, specifically how we can be sure we really "know" what we think we know. Both Descartes and Leibniz, like Plato so many centuries earlier, put our emotions and desires off to the side as potentially troubling distractions. These philosophers called on us to think as logically as possible, moving from unassailable assumptions to necessary conclusions, just as though human reality should be explored in the same abstract way as math.

Damasio makes the case that brain research itself indicates that whatever we mean by thinking is a far more complicated activity that cannot be divorced from what we are feeling.

Even the desire to solve a problem in mathematics (or work through a complex video game that is more than just pulling a trigger) is caught up in a web of emotional states. Many of us enjoy puzzles, for instance, because getting them right, especially faster than someone else, gives a nice endorphin boost. Depending on how addicted we are to the enterprise, being frustrated in the effort doesn't let us give up too soon. We still want that high.

Damasio is also the author of the book *Looking for Spinoza: Joy, Sorrow, and the Feeling Brain*. Spinoza stands out in the way he examines psychological states, and Damasio posits him as offering a corrective to

Descartes. A distinction Spinoza makes is between emotions, which can be visible to others, and feelings, which are strictly within our heads and are essentially the basis for how we act. When we talk about consciousness, we have to recognize it is something shared with much of the animal world so that we can assume an inner life that will to some degree resemble our own. With language we are able to share this with others of our kind, but what it is like for other creatures so far can only be guessed at.

WHAT IS A PERSON?

At a commonsense level we would not talk about someone (or something) as a person when there is not even the possibility of consciousness. We also think of consciousness as involving mental activity of some sort, and we usually consider this to involve whatever we mean by self-awareness (as Descartes clearly took for granted in his *cogito*). However, the concept of being a "person" also involves a notion of having legally respected rights and obligations, which is why a corporation such as IBM or an entity such as the city of Los Angeles can both sue and be sued in a court. Elsewhere in the world it extends even to natural features, such as a river (in India and New Zealand).

In the United States the issue of when we should consider a developing fetus to be a person is central to the controversy over legal abortions. In the Supreme Court decision that allowed a woman absolute choice over whether to continue or terminate her pregnancy prior to the time the fetus is viable (can live outside the uterus) it was acknowledged that there were no precedents in American law for an unborn child to be considered a person in this legal sense. For Catholics who believed an individual human soul to have been created at the moment of conception this was unacceptable, although for Jews traditionally it is only at birth that a living child is regarded as a person.

The Court, acknowledging both religious and scientific differences of opinion, stated that it was not the role of the Court to weigh in on this issue but instead maintained that for the first sixth months of pregnancy a government had no basis for interfering with a woman's decision. Could this change so that a "right to life" begins either at conception or relatively soon afterward? Theoretically it could, either by a new Court decision reversing *Roe v Wade* or by an amendment to the Constitution.

None of this, however, deals with the philosophical issue. Just what should we mean by "personhood" as an attribute for individual entities? Is the potential for consciousness a necessary condition? For a good part of the twentieth century in England and America, philosophers in the analytic tradition saw this, like other "metaphysical" questions, as "meaningless" in the sense that it was outside anything that science could deal with. This changed when in 1959 P.F. Strawson's book *Individuals: An Essay in Descriptive Metaphysics* appeared and opened a new chapter in the history of philosophical discussion.

What Strawson is doing is clearly a lot more than we can talk about in an introductory class, but one point has always stood out in my mind after my initial reading of his book many years back. Something has to be happening before we apply the term "person." If this has a definite beginning would it also have a definite end? Someone following Descartes would agree with the appearance of consciousness and self-awareness as marking a beginning, but what do we say as conscious capabilities decline (the case with Alzheimer's)? Am I still a person if I no longer know who I am? More to the point, what rights do I still have? Is personhood possibly a matter of degree?

In many ways I think the discussion is just beginning. As an example of what is happening now, I encourage you to explore the movement of Transhumanism, which suggests that instead of the traditional notion of an immortal soul we should talk about "patterns" that possibly can allow us to survive death through uploading to what we might call a cyberself.

WORKBOOK EXERCISES

Ryle attacks Descartes' logic by saying that his First Meditation involves a serious category mistake in its logic. What is that supposed mistake, and does this seem to be a valid criticism?

John Locke presented the interesting observation that if someone were to show up and seemingly had the memories of Socrates we would have to think of him as the same person as Socrates, just reborn. Memory, then, was for Locke a defining characteristic of personhood. How might this apply to someone convicted of murder and sentenced to death if in prison he were attacked and left with a permanent case of amnesia?

The philosophers Daniel Dennett and John Searles have both explored the question of personal identity with Dennett insisting that the sense I have of being "me" is essentially an illusion while Searle insists on its importance. Searles has attempted to make his point with what is called the Chinese Room example in which we are to imagine someone asked to translate from one language to another by matching up cards. His point is that being able to do this in no way indicates that the individual actually "knows" Chinese. Dennett strongly disagrees, insisting that there basically is no difference between the human translator and a computer program accomplishing the same task. What are your own thoughts here?

Philosophers since Plato have used thought experiments (the Allegory of the Cave, for instance), and in more recent writing we have examples such as the Brain in a Vat (an accident victim has been decapitated but his brain is preserved and artificially provided electronic impulses that simulate actual experiences) and the split brain hypothesis (brain tissue is somehow shared between two individuals so that they have the same past memories). The point is that the seeming reality of my memories and even present experiences is not enough to guarantee their authenticity. Would you agree?

A so-called postmodern approach to philosophy, expressed by American philosophers such as Richard Rorty, rejects the demand for certainty by reflecting on how we use language to establish a communal identity. On this basis we might have overlapping visions of reality, some useful and beneficial, others not. Does this appeal to you, or can you anticipate serious problems with what has been seen as "the substitution of solidarity for truth"?

6. A GREEK KING IS COMPARED TO HIS CHARIOT

Up to now I have been inviting you to look at philosophy as it has developed in the West as an entirely secular enterprise. Even when Jewish and Christian intellectuals in the early years of the Roman Empire adapted Plato's views to interpret their own religious teachings or Muslim intellectuals (and Thomas Aquinas) did the same with Aristotle, it was generally with the reservation that in any conflict between faith and reason it was faith that was to win out. By the time of Descartes the Catholic Church had come to accept the view of Thomas Aquinas that there really was no such conflict, but already advances in science were causing a wholesale rejection of philosophy as it had been seen in the Middle Ages. With the breakdown of any sense of religious unity philosophers were emboldened to talk about God and the soul in completely new ways.

While all this was going on in the West, over in Asia, especially in India, the study of what is objectively real and how we are to get at objective truth had been steadily advancing. One characteristic setting much of this apart from Western thinking was the idea that truth had different levels, depending on the readiness of the individual. Philosophy, then, did not really exist outside of a religious structure.

In India from an early stage there was the idea that the sacred scriptures known as the Vedas were to be the basis for any acceptable teaching, but unlike the situation in the West with the Bible or the Qur'an there was maximum leeway in how to interpret them. Eventually there would be three distinct approaches, each seen with one school more theoretical paired with another concentrating more on practice. Two of the resulting six schools that stand out are Vedanta and Samkhya.

The first is idealist in that a divine consciousness (*Brahman*) and our own consciousness (*atman*) are ultimately the same, while the other is the other dualist is that we are a linked *purusha* or spirit and *prakriti* or physical nature. They agree in saying that whatever we ordinarily understand to be ourselves (typically thought of as our minds or souls) do not outlast our physical bodies, even though there is something that carries on between lifetimes so that past actions (*karma*) determine a future setting. Both are considered orthodox Hindu traditions in that they are based on the Vedas.

In the fifth century BCE a holy man from Nepal, Siddhartha Gautama, presented a striking alternative to traditional Hinduism. Considered to be "enlightened" by his followers, he came to be called the Buddha. At the same time that Socrates, as Plato presents him, is offering a new vision of what it means to be human by seeing the soul as immortal, the Buddha is reframing the familiar Hindu belief in reincarnation to suggest that immortality is the problem, not the solution. Stripped to its most essential elements, his teaching was that (1) life is inevitably a matter of suffering (*dukkha*), (2) suffering is caused by our desires or cravings, (3) ending these cravings ends suffering, and (4) there is a specific path to follow in order to accomplish this.

What was most threatening about Buddhism to the powers-that-be in ancient India was its attack on the caste system that defined Hindu life. The Greek kings who remained in control of northwestern areas of India conquered by Alexander the Great understandably saw Buddhism as something they could exploit (much as Constantine exploited Christianity in the Roman Empire), and a legendary version of how this came about is the story of the meeting between King Milinda and the Buddhist teacher Nagasena. It is quite a remarkable document, but the key passage is what seems like a very irreverent exchange in which the Buddhist teacher appears to deny that there is really anyone present who would be either the king or the monk.

Pointing to the king's chariot we get an exhaustive listing of all its parts, none of which can be named as the chariot itself. In the same way we could list all the *skandhas* or characteristics of the two men and yet understand that any name we use (Milinda, Nagasena) would not refer to something separate from and so outlasting these characteristics.

BACK TO DESDCARTES FOR A MOMENT

In the *Meditations* Descartes had found it obvious that by being aware of his own thinking, even if it was the doubt he had about his supposed experience of a human body in a physical world, he could assert the existence of his mind as a reality in itself. Gilbert Ryle claimed this was a category mistake, like looking for the college as something separate from the buildings or classes or anything else we would see.

Nagasena is effectively carrying on the same disruptive analysis. Traditional Hindu thought (like traditional Western thought) asked about the substance underlying the appearances of anything we would see. Buddhism asserted that there was no such permanent physical reality (*nicca*) and certainly no permanent "soul" (*atta*). Buddhist teaching could then be summed up in these three words: *anicca, anatta, dukkha*.

Another way of looking at this is to see the difference between saying "**things** happen" and "things **happen**." It is natural enough to focus on the noun and not the verb, perhaps why the Greeks continued to think of fire as itself a thing and not a chemical process or happening. David Hume, reacting to Descartes, emphasized how our minds jump to concepts such as substance or cause and effect when in fact all we experience is a continuity or flow of impressions. Buddhist writers often point to Hume just as they do to contemporary physics, but the difference is that neither Hume nor Stephen Hawking buy into the idea of reincarnation. For the Buddhist there is the conviction, taken on faith, that unless we do something about it we get to ride the merry-go-round over and over, long after it has ceased being fun.

WORKBOOK EXERCISES

Descartes simply equates the concepts of "mind" and "soul" in the Meditations. How would they be separated in Indian thought?

Plato accepts the idea of reincarnation while admitting that it is not something he can prove. In Hinduism the idea is also a given, important in that it provides justification for the caste system. Why would it not appear in any other of the Western philosophers we have met?

Some recent writers have come to point out the bias of American philosophy departments in not providing any serious exposure to Asian views. One suggested example of where this matters is that in the West we think of time in a linear manner, somehow beginning and ending, while in Asian views the image is not that of a line but of a circle. How might this affect a cultural understanding of progress? How might it also affect talking about the goals of philosophy itself?

7. EXISTENTIALISM AND THE PROBLEMS OF FREEDOM AND AUTHENTICITY

 A view of science as essentially dealing with who and what we are strictly from the outside, as in the rise of behavioral psychology late in the nineteenth century, triggered a philosophical call to create a new science of consciousness based on our subjective experiences. As presented by Edmund Husserl, philosophers, instead of surrendering their role to the new "positivism," should focus on the actual presentations or phenomena in our experience. This he called phenomenology with its key being an effort to describe the very thing science would put aside: how does it feel to be in a situation?

One of the writers taking this to heart was Jean-Paul Sartre, teaching in Paris at the time of Nazi occupation. In 1943 he published *Being and Nothingness: An Essay on Phenomenological Ontology.* By this time the German philosopher Martin Heidegger, also following Husserl's lead, had written *Being and Time* in which he puts emphasis on the individual's "being there" with the term *dasein*, now translated as "existence." Attempting to explain his own approach, Sartre takes over the term "existentialism," but he also decides to use novels, short stories, and plays as a more convenient way of presenting his key views. This created a vogue in the postwar period, not just in Europe but in America. In his highly successful play "No Exit," for example, he deals with the issues of freedom and personal integrity or authenticity by having three characters put together in a hotel room that represents the afterlife as it will be for them ("Hell is other people").

Central to his thinking is the idea that each of us has the radical freedom to take charge of our lives. The failure of philosophers to make an air-tight case for the existence of God left the individual in the personal position either to make the jump of faith or accept a reality in which God was now totally absent. His own approach was that any traditional belief in God effectively compromised the idea of free will, so he chose atheism.

55

The consequence was that there was no divine blueprint for how to live. However, for Sartre this also implied that if I make a moral choice for myself I must be thinking how this defines humanity itself, as though I am saying how I would want everyone to live. If I choose to lie or steal, then it has to be acceptable for everyone else to be liars or thieves.

Obviously most of us never act this way. Typically we might accept a certain rule of behavior but make exceptions for ourselves. This Sartre calls "bad faith," and it played a role in his discussion of anti-Semitism and its denial of Jews being "human" when the Nazi government declared them as somehow subhuman and their lives and property no longer legally protected. He and his colleague Albert Camus, who also used literature as a vehicle, pushed the idea that my personal choice to live rather than commit suicide (seen as a logical response to being marooned in a world without meaning) meant I had to respect other lives as well and act accordingly (for Camus, even if this meant being willing to kill a former friend who had become a Nazi).

In an essay Sartre tried to explain what all this meant in practice. He talks about a student coming to see him during the war. The young man's friends were already planning to escape France and meet up with the forces planning to take their country back from the Germans. His own dilemma was that he was the only support for his mother, and escaping would most likely mean her death. What should he do? Sartre makes the point that in this dilemma there was no way of talking about a "right" choice. The student would have to say whom he loved more, his mother or his country, by the choice he actually made.

Sartre himself was involved in the Resistance, but another of his colleagues, Maurice Merleau-Ponty, challenged him on the hard line he took about facing up to the Nazis. The only true patriot, it seemed had to be someone just standing in the path of the tanks and giving up his life for his cause. Realistically, there was no way to live in history and, as he said, still have clean hands.

Sartre eventually did back away from the view that anyone not choosing with the intensity he expected must be acting in bad faith. Perfect authenticity might still be an ideal, but most of us would never be up to the challenge.

OTHER IMPORTANT EXISTENTIALISTS

Sartre and Camus with their almost ideological atheism came to equate existentialism in the public mind with a denial of God. However, there were to be a number of philosophers who shared the existentialist emphasis on the individual but saw a positive role for religion.

Karl Jaspers, a German married to a Jewish woman and because of that living in fear during the war, had begun as a psychiatrist before moving on to philosophy. He attempted to call attention to what it meant to be "encompassed" in a greater reality, as in his statement that "the man who attains true awareness of his freedom gains certainty of God."

In France there was the Catholic Gabriel Marcel, whose view of Christianity led him to write about a "creative fidelity" in opposition to the dehumanizing tendencies of technology. From Germany again was also the Jewish philosopher Martin Buber, best known for stressing a distinction between I-It and I-Thou relationships.

What all these writers had in common was an emphasis on examining the contents of conscious awareness with a particular focus on how we make our choices. An overly simplistic contrast between existentialists (such as Sartre) and behaviorists (such as Skinner) is that for the existentialist we are free but in bad faith try to say we are conditioned while the behaviorist argues we are not free but conditioned for societal purposes to say we are.

WORKBOOK EXERCISES

How did advocates of phenomenology attempt to redirect talking about human consciousness?

For writers like Sartre and Camus, what followed from the deliberate choice not to believe in God?

As time went on and memories of Nazi occupation and the Holocaust faded, the existentialist emphasis on individual responsibility did as well. Is there evidence that the existentialist vision of human equality is fading as well?

8.   REDEFINING (STILL AGAIN) THE JOB OF PHILOSOPHY

Ludwig Wittgenstein as an individual is possibly the most striking exception we have ever seen to whatever mental image we might have of a world-famous philosopher. His first book established his reputation in the field of symbolic logic (he's the one who came up with truth tables as a test for deductive validity), but when war broke out in 1914 he enlisted in the Austrian army in part to test himself and afterward virtually disappeared to teach small children in a remote village. When he returned to academic life his lectures and the notes published after his death as *Philosophical Investigations* essentially rewrote how to talk about talking. His concept of language games stressed that the meaning of what we say is essentially to be understood in terms of usage rather than an imagined correspondence with an exterior reality. What this suggests for what we do in this course is expressed in his aphorism that "philosophy is a battle against the bewitchment of our intelligence by means of language."

One example of how Wittgenstein asks us to shift our attention is in a question about irrational numbers, such as *pi* (how many times the diameter of any circle can be fit into its circumference). There is an algorithm to carry out the process by which we move past 3.1412 to an unlimited number of digits (presently computers have taken this into the trillions). Now, does God know whether we ever get to a point where the same number keeps reappearing (as when 1/3 becomes .3333...)? For Wittgenstein, this is not at all a question about God or divine knowledge, and it is not even a question about *pi*. His point is that numbers, and that means all numbers including ones like *pi*, are essentially human inventions and we cannot talk about them as existing apart from our own thought processes.

The most important point he wants to make when he talks about language games is the very problem of saying what counts as a game. Examined carefully, we see that we call something a game not because of a common characteristic but because of a similarity to something we already call a game. The parallel is with what might happen at a family reunion, where some individuals obviously have the same chins, others the same eyes, and others the same ears, but there is no one characteristic they all share. What we can then say about many of our terms is that there is a family resemblance. The confusion sets in when we are looking for something more.

This takes us full circle back to where we began in this course when we looked at Plato and the "truth" of the Pythagorean Theorem. Plato reasoned (as did the German philosopher Kant many centuries later) that through mathematics we had access to a knowledge independent of physical experience. This was the foundation of his own approach to both knowledge and reality. Wittgenstein, otherwise so important in the history of modern logic, makes us back up and stop cold. Like Bertrand Russell, his own mentor, we have to watch the confines that language itself creates for our questions.

CONCEPTS AND CONSTRUCTS

In the Middle Ages debates about God often centered on the concept of *possibilia*, whatever might exist. One of the intriguing moves in contemporary metaphysics has been the argument of the philosopher David Lewis that whatever could happen with infinite possibilities actually has to be true of some alternate world. The German philosopher Leibniz a few centuries earlier argued that the very concept of God implied that this is the best of all possible worlds, and traditionally the problem of evil has been resolved by thinking of God as a playwright who comes up with the best possible script.

Wittgenstein would clearly have us walk away from this kind of intellectual puzzle. One way of sorting things out has been to make a clear distinction between concepts and constructs. If we follow John Locke and David Hume, we build our concepts (our ideas of cabbages and kings) from the ground up as we talk about our sensory impressions. The variability in how we can do this has been pointed out by the philosopher Willard Quine in his *gavagai* example: imagine anthropologists seeing a rabbit jumping along and are told by natives that this is *gavagai*, but what is not clear is whether this refers to the type of animal, to the kind of thing the animal is doing, or to the part of the animal that stands out in its jumping.

Now we want to explain how all this fits together as we build a framework of some sorts. We use analogies to have old terms used in new ways. For example, we talk about "atoms," not that long back imagined like tiny solar systems with electrons orbiting around a nucleus. As time goes on we have moved away from talking about electrons as things and instead thought of them as events, and in still further developments we are best advised to leave our imaginations alone and keep to equations. To mark what we have done we might use the term "construct," which reflects the building process involved.

WORKBOOK EXERCISES

What does Wittgenstein have in mind when talks about language games? Is he suggesting that philosophical definitions are useless?

What are factors that might contribute to the fact that philosophers never seem to reach a consensus?

Printed in Great
Britain
by Amazon

31041101R00038